**THE GET ALONG GANG™ ANNUAL 1986** Published by Marvel Comics Ltd. in association with Grandreams Ltd. Office of publication: 23 Redan Place, London W2 4SA.  Printed in Holland. 

**Edited and compiled by Jenny O'Connor.**

ISBN 0 86227 375 7

**£3.50**

GUMMY FOOT SWAMP
THE GANG ARE PLAYING GAMES IN THEIR WARM CLUBHOUSE, WHILE I'M STUCK IN A DAMP DEN IN THE SWAMP!
ERK!
SLIP!
SKID!
THE COLD SNAP'S MADE HIS MACHINE SKID! I FEEL LIKE SCARING HIM WITH ANOTHER SNAP!
OLD TROLL BRIDGE
MY BOX OF TRICKS... SAVED!
SKID!!
YOU SHALL BE REWARDED I SHALL PUT MY SPECIAL TALENTS AT YOUR DISPOSAL!
WHAT ARE THEY, THEN?
HMM... I FEEL A MEAN, SNEAKY IDEA COMING ON!
RUB!!!!

I'LL FETCH MY ROULETTE WHEEL!
PERFECT!
I'M AFTER YOU... GNASH!
HUH? CATCHUM CAN'T CATCH ME!
ENJOY YOUR TRIP? SNEK: SNEK!
TRIP!
BACK AT CATCHUM'S DEN...
INTRODUCING DOCTOR PANDA MONIUM AND HIS BOX OF TRICKS!
FIDDLE!
BINGO ONE, MEET BINGO TWO! YOUR FULLY AUTOMATED ROBOT!
CAN'T CATCH ME!
WHIRL!
FWD.
HERE COMES BINGO AT A HECK OF A RATE!
CAN'T CATCH ME!
SKIP

HUH... STOP, WHAT'S GOT INTO...
CAN'T CATCH ME...
...YOU...OOOCH!
CAN'T CATCH ME!
I'LL GET BACK TO THE DEN. IT'S CHILLY OUT HERE!
MAYBE. BUT I'LL MAKE THINGS HOT FOR THAT PESKY GANG!
READY TO TRY THE NEXT CHEER LEADING ROUTINE, TWO, FOUR, SIX, EIGHT...
HERE'S BINGO. WONDER WHAT TOOK HIM SO LONG?
CAN'T CATCH ME!
YIPES!
EEEK!
AAAGH!
RACE YOU TO HOOF'S AND BACK, MONTGOMERY.
ON YOUR MARKS, GET SET...
CAN'T CATCH ME!

WAAH!
CAN'T CATCH ME...
CRASH!!!
GOOOUUCH!
HE'S GONE TOO FAR THIS TIME!
SO SAY ALL OF US. AFTER HIM!
HE'LL CATCH IT FROM US FOR THIS! HE CAN'T RUN FOREVER!
I'LL SET THE CONTROL TO STRAIGHT ON-INFINITY. HE'LL NEVER STOP!
STRAIGHT ON INDIFINATELY
BACKWARDS
AND WHILE THEY'RE OFF CHASING HIM, I'LL LOAD ALL THEIR GAMES AND TOYS ON TO MY CARTIE!
THERE MUST BE SOMETHING THE MATTER WITH HIM. WE'LL FIND OUT, IF WE CAN STOP HIM!
CAN'T CATCH ME!
ONLY ONE WAY TO DO THAT!
ROPED HIM... BUT I CAN'T STOP HIM. LEND A HAND, GANG!

WE'VE CAUGHT HIM, BUT WE CAN'T STOP HIM... UNLESS...
CAN'T CATCH ME!
WRAP THE ROPE AROUND THAT TREE TRUNK...
IT'S WORKING, HE'S BEING PULLEY ROUND IN CIRCLES!
ERK! BINGO'S ON THE LOOSE AGAIN!
I'M NOT SO SURE IT IS BINGO... HEAR THAT FUNNY WHIRRING SOUND?
SNAP!!!
WHIR!!
WHIR!!
THE BEAV-O-BOT AND THE GANG WILL BE MILES AWAY BY NOW. SOON HAVE THEIR GAMES BACK IN OUR DEN!
PUZZLE
MONOTONY
CAN'T CATCH ME!
BLEEP!!
BLEEP!!!
WHIR!!
MONOTONY
SNAKES & LADDERS
WHAT... WAAAAAH!

GOT TO STOP THIS THING... GOT TO USE THE CONTROLS!
CAN'T CATCH ME!
SWAMP
CONTROLS... THAT BEAVER... IT'S A ROBOT!
CAN'T CATCH ME!
GUMMY FOOT SWAMP
WAAAH! LELAND!
SOUNDS LIKE CATCHUM BACK WITH YOUR GAMES. YOU CAN WATCH US PLAY WITH THEM BEFORE WE SMASH THEM UP!
PERHAPS I SHOULDN'T HAVE GIVEN YOU THAT BEAVO-BOT AS A REWARD! I'M GOING!
GOOWCH!
CRASH!
YOU'RE THE LIGHTEST, BRAKER, SO YOU CAN CROSS THE ICE TO CATCHUM'S DEN!
UGH... BOSS WHAT'S HAPPENED...?
CAN'T CATCH ME!
THANKS, PAL... NOW LET'S GET OUT OF HERE!

AAAGH. BINGO'S SHUT THE BEAVO-BOT IN HERE WITH US! I'VE LOST THE CONTROLS... CAN'T STOP IT!
LEAVE IT TO ME, BOSS!
WHIR!!
BLEEP
YOU MISSED AND SMASHED A HOLE IN THE FLOOR... THE DEN'S SINKING!
YOU... YOU GRR... TAKE THIS!
CAN'T CATCH ME...
LET'S GET-ALONG TO THE CABOOSE AND PLAY A GAME OF MONOTONY!
WHAT HAVE I DONE. THAT'S OFFICER GROWLER!
SPLUDGE!
THIS CARD SAYS I HAVE TO GO TO JAIL!
IT'S JUST A GAME, BINGO!
GO TO JAIL
NOT FOR SOME. CATCHUM'S COPPED IT!
JAIL
GO TO JAIL!
END.

# BINGO'S PICTURE PUZZLE

How well do you know the gang? See if you can fill in the names of the five characters by using the clues!

1. | | | | | |

2. Z I P P E R

3. p o r t i d

4. | | | | | |

5. D O T T Y

LAMPITT & BRADSHAW.

SPO
BUTTE
The Get Along Ga
spotting butterfli
the fun too! How
can you see?
counte
co
LAMPITT & BRADSHAW.

ING
FLIES!
t
n join in
terflies
have
vhy not
n in!
D

# GOODBYE CLUBHOUSE CABOOSE!

**Catchum Crocodile beamed a mischievous smile. "The Mayor wants to keep Green Meadow beautiful and tidy. If we tell him what an eyesore the Caboose is, he'll get rid of it!"**

**PLIP! PLOP! PLIP! PLOP!** "Hey, who's flicking water over me?" demanded Rudyard as he felt drops of cold water trickling down his nose.

The Gang were relaxing in the Clubhouse Caboose, keeping out of the rain. They looked up at Rudyard's cry and tried to hide their grins.

"It's not us, you loopy lion," chuckled Zipper, putting down his sport book. "The rain's coming in through a hole in the roof and you're standing under it!"

The others started to laugh at their friend's mistake but suddenly their faces fell in alarm.

"**JEEPERS**! Why are we laughing? A hole in the Caboose roof? That's terrible! All my sweets will get wet!" wailed Lolly.

"Never mind your sweets, what about my photograph collection?" said a worried Flora.

"And my books," piped up Braker.

"Quickly, get a bucket to catch the rain," said Dotty, taking charge. "Or the Caboose will be flooded!"

When the rain finally stopped, the Gang looked at the roof.

"It's a large hole," frowned Montgomery. "We're going to have to fix it before another rainshower arrives."

While Bernice mopped up the water that had spilled from the full bucket, the others set to work outside.

"I'll go on the roof," said Bingo, snatching the ladder from Rocco. "I'll bet I make a good job of fixing it too."

"You mean I will!" snapped Zipper, pulling the ladder away from his friend. "I like climbing almost as much as I like running."

"Why can't I do it?" asked Portia.

"Don't be silly," snorted Rocco. "This isn't a job for a girl!"

"Hold it!" Braker quickly put the brakes on any more squabbles. "If we start arguing now, we'll never get the job done."

"Braker's right," agreed Montgomery. "To keep the peace let's all go onto the roof."

"Er, do you think the roof is strong enough to hold all of us?" Flora asked nervously after everyone had scrambled to the top of the Caboose.

"I'm... not... sure," replied Montgomery slowly. He was beginning to suspect his idea wasn't such a clever one after all. "Maybe we should all climb down again and think of something else?"

Before Montgomery could suggest this to the others, the roof collapsed under their weight.

**KRRRRAAAAAAAASSSSSSHH!**

"**WAAAAAAAAAHHHHH!**" they all screamed as they tumbled into the Caboose.

**FLUMPH!**

"Goodness!" Bernice gasped as the Gang landed beside her feet. "Why didn't you use the door like you usually do?"

"Ha. Ha. Very funny," groaned Zipper, struggling free of the pile of bodies. Then he looked at the **huge** hole that had now appeared in the roof. "Oh no! It's worse than ever. Now what are we going to do?"

"Cor, Catchum, don't the Gang's Caboose look a mess?" Leland Lizard gave a wheezy chuckle as he trotted by the

Caboose with his best pal, Catchum Crocodile. The two pests had spent the morning pilfering jam tarts from Mrs Bun's cake shop. This was great fun until she caught them and gave their hands a hard slap with her wooden cooking spoon. Now they were heading home for dinner.

Catchum beamed a mischievous smile as he saw the sorry state the Caboose was in. "Yes, it is a mess. In fact it's an eyesore. I think we should tell the Mayor about this."

Leland, who wasn't too bright at the best of times, scratched his bald head and looked puzzled. "What's the Mayor got to do with it?" he asked.

Catchum rapped his fist on Leland's head. "Nitwit! I sometimes wonder if you have any brains in there at all! The Mayor wants to keep Green Meadow beautiful and tidy. If we tell him what an eyesore the Caboose is, he'll get rid of it! **HAW! HAW! HAW!**"

"We can't do anything about the hole now," Montgomery was telling the others. "We promised Mr Hoofnagel we would paint the outside of the shop and the Get Along Gang never break a promise."

Bingo grinned, rubbing his stomach in expectation. "Especially

not when Mr Hoofnagel's offered us free ice-creams afterwards!" he laughed.

Montgomery sighed. He sometimes wondered about his friend's good intentions.

"Shouldn't we cover the hole with something?" suggested Rudyard. "It does look a bit of a mess."

Dotty shook her head. "We don't have time. Anyway, nothing's going to happen to the Caboose while we're away."

The Gang returned from Mr Hoofnagel's that afternoon to discover... "**EEEEEP! SOMEONE'S STOLEN OUR CABOOSE!**" squealed Flora, looking at the empty space where the Caboose had once stood.

"Let's fetch Officer Growler! He'll track down the thief!" said Rocco.

"Excuse me," said a deep voice behind them. "Your Caboose hasn't been stolen. I've sent it to the scrap-yard."

The Gang turned around to find the Mayor standing near them.

"**WHAAAAT?!**" roared Zipper angrily. "Why did you do that?"

"The Caboose was in a dreadful state," the Mayor explained. "That young Catchum Crocodile was quite right in asking me to remove it."

"**CATCHUM!**" Rudyard bellowed.

"He **would** be behind this!"

"You'll just have to find somewhere else to meet. Now I'm off to the Town Hall to unveil a statue of myself. Goodbye." With that, the Mayor, who was rather fat, waddled off towards the town centre.

"This would never have happened if we hadn't fallen out," moaned Woolma.

"Our lovely Caboose, gone forever," wailed Flora. "How awful!"

"Oh, no it isn't," said Montgomery determinedly. "We're going to get it back and fix it until it looks like it's brand new. Then the Mayor will **have** to let us keep it!"

"Ooh! Ooh! Catchum, look!" Leland nudged his friend as they drove past the scrap-yard in their tatty cartie. Catchum stared in disbelief as he saw the Gang inside the scrap-yard struggling to push their Caboose out onto the street.

"This is a dream come true!" he cackled, slapping Leland hard on the back and knocking all the breath out of him. "I've finally caught the Gang red-handed – doing something wrong! Quick! Let's find the Mayor and tell him!" Catchum could not believe his luck. He would get praised for telling tales on them and the Gang would land in hot water for once. "Oh, happy days are here again!" he sang as Leland drove him towards the Town Hall.

"Come on Gang, **PUSH!**" urged Dotty with her cheerleader spirit as they all struggled to move the Caboose. "Catchum's just ridden past. He's probably dashed off to get us into more bother."

With one extra mighty team push, the Caboose rolled easily onto the pavement. Montgomery looked worried as the Gang pushed it along the street. "To return the Clubhouse back where it belongs we'll have to go past the Town Hall."

Zipper tried to keep a straight face as he said, "Why, old chum, do you think someone might see us?" This made the others laugh.

"You twit, Zipper," smiled Portia. "But that's why I love the Gang. Even when we have problems we can laugh about them."

"Hurry, Leland, hurry!" Catchum shook his friend hard, urging him to drive the cartie faster.

"I'm doing my best, boss," Leland grumbled. "But this rotten cartie's falling to pieces. You're too mean to pay out and get it repaired!"

**SNAP!**

As Leland spoke, the cartie's wooden brake lever snapped off in his hand. "Yipes! Now we can't stop!" he yelled as the cartie sped downhill to where the Mayor and the townsfolk were gathered. "We're gonna crash!"

The Gang had reached the town centre. They were wondering how to get past the crowd gathered near the Town Hall when they saw the cartie hurtling towards the Mayor's statue.

"If we don't stop it, the statue will be demolished! **PUSH!**" Montgomery ordered his friends.

Using all their strength, the Gang succeeded in pushing the Caboose in front of the statue before the cartie arrived.

**SMAAA-ASSH!**

"**WARGLE!**" gasped Catchum and Leland as the cartie crashed into the side of the Caboose and they were thrown clear.

"Well done!" the Mayor praised the Gang. "You've saved my statue!"

"We couldn't have done it without our Caboose," Bernice reminded him. The Mayor smiled. "You're quite right and I've changed my mind. You can keep the Caboose after all – and Catchum and Leland will fix it for you."

"We will not!" roared Catchum angrily. "Let the twits do it themselves!"

"You'll mend it or you'll spend a day in prison for dangerous driving!" The Mayor winked at the Gang as if to say, "I'm only joking!" but Catchum didn't know this.

"Er, let's get started, pal," Catchum grinned sheepishly at Leland and the two friends set to work.

"Ha! Ha! Fancy Catchum helping us," chuckled Rocco. "This **is** a day to remember!"

Dotty and Zipper play . . .

# checks!

## A Game for two players!

All you need is a dice and two different colouring pens. Take it in turns to throw the dice. Then colour in the number of squares you have thrown. When the page has been completely coloured, count up.

GET ALONG GANG IN...
MAKING TRACKS!
SOON HAVE THIS SNOWMAN BUILT!
THE GET ALONG GANG — WORKING TOGETHER — AS A TEAM!
THERE, YOUNG CHIPMUNKS, A SNOW-MAN COURTESY OF THE GET ALONG GANG.
THINKING OF OTHERS, TOO!
GAH! MY HAT, MY TRUNCHEON, MY BOOTS! WHO BUILT THAT SNOWMAN!
THEY MADE IT!
WE'D BETTER GET ALONG, GANG — FAST
ENERGETIC, TOO! I'VE SEEN ENOUGH!
OH, NO. MORE TROUBLE WHO HAVE WE UPSET NOW?
BOK!
WHOOPS!

BOW
MAC THE YAK, WORLD WIDE CAMERMAN! FANCY WINGING AWAY FROM ALL THIS ON A PHOTOGRAPHIC ASSIGNMENT?
SOMEWHERE EXOTIC I HOPE, FOR A PHOTO SESSION I'LL LOOK MY BEST!
THAT BAD, EH, WOOLMA. BUT COUNT US IN. WE LOVE ADVENTURE, AND GREEN MEADOWS!
AND SO, DAYS LATER...
THE YAK HAS BROUGHT US ALL THE WAY TO TIBET!
SNAP
BRR! I JUST CAN'T GET ANY COLDER!
EEEEK!
WANT T' BET? HEE, HEE!
I AM MAC THE YAK. WHO WILL JOIN ME AS I SEARCH THE MOUNTAIN WASTES!
NONE OF US LOT, MAC.
THE GANG WILL STICK WITH HIM LIKE WE STICK WITH EACH OTHER!
IT'S SNOWING AND IT'S BOUND TO GET WINDY TOO!
WOOOOAAAAR!
I CAN HEAR THE WIND ROARING ALREADY!
I DON'T THINK THAT'S THE WIND, WOOLMA!

WHAT'S THAT? SHOOTING STAR? METEORITE?
IT LOOKED LIKE A GIANT SNOW-BALL TO ME!
HEAR THAT? JUST AS I WAS FEELING PECKISH, MAC'S SUGGESTED WE "HAVE LUNCH"!
WHOOOOSH!
NOT "HAVE LUNCH", BINGO... I WAS YELLING...
...AVALANCHE! INTO THAT CAVE, GANG!
WELL HERE WE ARE, SNOWED UP IN SOME CAVE... AND NOT A SINGLE PHOTO FROM YOU YET!
WE HAVEN'T SEEN A SINGLE SNOWMAN YET!
THE ABOMINABLE KIND OF COURSE. ALSO KNOWN AS THE YETI! THAT ROARING, THE AVALANCHE, SOME FURRY FIEND AT WORK!
YOU MEAN YOU'VE COME TO TRACK DOWN AN ABOMINABLE SNOWMAN?

KEEP SPINNING HIM ROUND, GANG!
JUST' COS I'VE GOT THE BIGGEST ANTLERS, I HAVE TO DO THE BORING WORK!
PERHAPS A PICTURE OF MY INTREPID TEAM.
TWO WAYS ROUND. I SAY WE GO RIGHT!
WHAT'S WRONG WITH LEFT?
BACK A BIT, BACK A BIT...
FLUMP!
PERFECT... UUUGH?
WE'LL LOOK THIS WAY FOR HIM... YOU CHECK OUT THE LEFT HAND ROUTE! TUG ON THE ROPE IF YOU FIND ANYTHING!
AND...
HEY! MASSIVE FOOTPRINTS MAC MUST HAVE FOLLOWED THEM... GIVE THE ROPE A TUG TO TELL THE OTHERS!

CONTINUED ON PAGE 41...

JANUARY 1987
1. Start here! Throw a 6 to start!
2.
3. Dotty cheerleads! On 2!
4. 1st sunny day! On 1
5.
8.
9. Top of the class! On 3!
10.
11. Party! On 2!
12.
15 Zipper wins sport's day. On 5!
16.
17. Row! Back 1!
18.
19.
22.
23. Ballet lesson! On 3!
24.
25. Friends again. On 3!
26.
29. Library! On 1!
30.
31. Well done! You've made it!
LAMPITT & BRADSHAW.

# THE CALENDAR GAME!

Play the Calendar game and see what the gang are up to in January. Any number of people can play. All you need is some dice and some counters or buttons. Throw a six to start. First to January 31st, wins the game!

P
D
LAMPITT & BRADSHAW.

# rtia's Paperchase!

Portia has laid a paperchase trail for the Gang to follow. Join in the rough and tumble and play the Paperchase Game! All you need to play is a dice and some coloured pens! Chose a Gang member to play with. The object of the game is to collect as many pieces of paper you can for your partner. Take it in turns to throw the dice. The number you throw tells you how many pieces of paper you can colour in your own colour. When all the paper has been coloured, do a count up and see who has won!

# ODD JOBS!

**There's trouble when the Gang decide to earn some money in the school holiday!**

"Ho hum. We're broke again," Braker sighed, emptying out the Gang's piggy bank onto the Caboose table. "All we've saved up is twenty seven pence and three bingo tokens."

Bingo's face went red with embarrassment at this. "I wonder how they got there?" he said, trying hard to look innocent.

Every week, the Gang contributed some of their pocket-money to the piggy bank to save up for a day when they needed it most. But recently, Bingo had been slipping tokens into the bank instead, so that he could treat himself to an extra bag of sweets each week.

The Gang scowled at their friend but they had more pressing matters to concern them.

"That's a nuisance. We girls were going to buy a new computer game," said Dotty, looking disappointed.

Montgomery frowned when he heard this. "You mean we boys had plans to buy a new set of lights for our bikes," he said huffily.

Bernice interrupted them. "Let's not argue about it now. What we need is a part-time job to earn some money." Everyone thought this was a good idea. "But any money we make will go towards buying a computer game," Bernice finished quickly.

"Bike lights, you mean!" snapped Rocco.

**"WE'LL SEE ABOUT THAT!"** the Gang shouted at once, and all hurried from the Caboose to be the first to find a holiday job.

**"WANTED. DELIVERY HELPERS"** read the sign outside Mr Opple's vegetable shop. "That's for us!" cheered the girls, running towards the open doorway.

"Quick! The girls are going to pinch our jobs!" shouted Rudyard. The boys dashed after them and reached the door at the same time.

"Move over! We were here first!" Lolly cried as they all tried to get inside the shop at the same time.

"Shut up!" snapped Rocco. "We've got just as much right to the job as you!"

"Stop mucking about!" called Mr Opple from inside his shop. "You're blocking my doorway. My customers can't get in."

The Gang tried to move backwards. Then they tried to push forwards, but it was no use. They had managed to wedge themselves tightly in the doorway.

"Oh, lummy! We're stuck!" squeaked Woolma. "And you lot are crushing my pretty dress!"

Mr Opple wasn't amused. "Pesky kids! Here, let me help." He pushed at the Gang as hard as he could.

**"WAAAH!"** yelped Portia, as they fell back into the street. Woolma crashed into a cart outside the shop, sending boxes of apples tumbling down the road.

"Ooops! That's upset the apple cart!" the little lamb grinned sheepishly.

After picking up all the apples and apologising to an angry Mr Opple, the Gang hurried off before they landed up in any more trouble.

"That's your fault!" Montgomery accused the girls.

"You boys cost us that job!" Dotty said huffily.

"I'll hire you all on a trial period," Mr Bullwhip told the Gang in his ironmongers shop. "Whoever does the best work can have the holiday job."

He told them to move a stack of paint-tins to the back of the shop. In their eagerness, both Zipper and Lolly picked-up the same tin.

"S'mine!" growled Zipper, struggling to pull the tin away from Lolly.

"Lolly had it first!" shouted Portia, watching as her friend snatched the tin away from Zipper. Suddenly the tin fell out of her hands and onto the

floor. The lid slipped off and green paint ran all over the place.

**"OUT! OUT!"** roared Mr Bullwhip when he discovered the mess. "I don't want **any** of you working here! You're all useless!"

"There must be a holiday job we can do without the girls knowing," Montgomery muttered sourly as the boys walked along the street later on that day. "We'll do **anything!"**

Rudyard pulled on Montgomery's jumper. "Look there! That's for us!" A notice in the window of a clothes shop read, **HELP WANTED.**

Braker wasn't so sure. "Shouldn't we find out what it is first?"

Bingo frowned at his friend. "You're always putting the brakes on good ideas. Just shut-up and don't argue. The girls might take it if we don't hurry."

"Are you **sure** you want this job?" asked a surprised shop manager after the boys had approached him.

"We don't care what it is," said Montgomery. "Anything at all."

"All right," agreed the manager, who still couldn't believe his ears. "Go and change into your outfits."

"Gosh! A job **and** smart new outfits," Zipper smiled. "I wonder what they look like?"

"A cleaning job? We'll take it!" Dotty told the garage owner.

"Yes, I'm an expert at cleaning," agreed Bernice.

The garage owner looked puzzled. "You're eager enough, but I don't know . . ."

"Oh, please give us a job," pleaded Portia. "We're hard workers."

"Okay, I'll give you a try," the garage owner grinned.

"I wonder what the job is," Flora said as the girls followed their new boss to the back of the garage.

"It can't be much," smiled Lolly. "Probably cleaning up a few sweet papers or something."

"OOH, I FEEL SUCH A FOOL!" Montgomery stood in the centre of the shop with the rest of the boys. He was wearing a pretty pink straw hat and a yellow polka dot dress. His friends were also wearing girls' hats, dresses and shoes. Rudyard and Rocco were holding handbags as well. Laughing customers had surrounded the boys.

"Ooooh! Don't they look sweet!" called out one of Zipper's chums.

Zipper cringed at this. "I'll never live this down!" he groaned.

Braker was not at all happy in the purple evening-gown he was wearing. "Hummph! I knew we should have found out what the job was first!"

"How was I to know it was a girls' fashion-show?" Rudyard complained, trying to hide behind the others so that no-one could see him.

"I bet the girls have got a better job than this," Bingo grumbled. "They're probably laughing at us right now."

"URRGH! I'm covered in oil!" Woolma threw down the box of tools she was struggling to carry in disgust! Her face, arms and legs were thick with black, sticky oil.

"Who was daft enough to get us this job?" snapped Dotty as she stepped into another pool of oil. She quickly went quiet as she realised that she was to blame.

"I don't know," said Lolly smiling. "I haven't got dirty yet." This was true. Lolly was as clean as when she had entered the garage.

Portia scowled. "But you have the knack of staying clean no matter what!"

Cleaning car-engines and mopping-up oil isn't my idea of fun either," said Bernice, throwing down the oil-covered broom. "Let's quit and find the boys. It's about time we started working together."

"Ha! Ha! I wish we had seen your fashion-show," giggled Portia, after the boys had told their friends what had happened. "You must have looked funny!"

Montgomery couldn't help grinning. "We did feel right twits, but it will teach us not to try and beat you girls. The Get Along Gang should work together."

"Yes, we'll share any money we make," agreed Dotty.

Just then, Lolly, who had been out hunting for a holiday job that they could all do together, rushed into the Caboose.

"Hey, Gang, my dad's looking for sweet-tasters at his factory! Come on!"

Catchum and Leland had also heard of the job. "Hurry!" Catchum urged his friend as they drove towards the factory in their cartie. "Even just thinking about all those sweets I'm going to scoff is making my tummy rumble!"

Catchum's face fell as he saw the Gang running towards the factory. **"AARRRGGH!** Those rotters are gonna pinch my lovely job! **Stop 'em!"**

**WHAM!**

Leland drove the cartie into the Gang. **"WAAAROO!"** they yelled as

they went hurtling into the air.

They landed on top of a pig who was wearing a **SCHNEIDER'S SWEET FACTORY** overall and carrying a large sack.

"Oh, crikey! We've knocked out one of the factory workers," frowned Braker, looking down at the dazed pig beneath them.

"Who did this?" demanded Lolly's dad as he came hurrying up and pointed to the pig.

Montgomery, who never told fibs, sighed. "We did," he said sadly.

**"HAW!** The Gang's in trouble now!" cackled Catchum. "The job's as good as mine!"

To the Gang's surprise, Lolly's dad beamed happily. "Well done! This thief disguised himself as one of my workers to rob my factory." He held up the bag which was full of sweets. "He would have got away with it too if you hadn't stopped him. If you want the sweet-tasters' jobs, they're yours.

**"YAAAAY!"** cheered the Gang.

"Bah! Humbug! Foiled again!" cursed Catchum.

The Gang settled down to their new job. "Being paid to do what we do best," chuckled Lolly. "That's what I call the **SWEET** taste of success!"

# POP DOTS!

What a sound! The Pop Alongs have got together to play for you! Can you guess which instrument each one is playing? Join up the dots starting at number 1 each time, and make your band complete. Once you have completed the picture, you can colour in the instruments too!

# Bingo's Po

Bingo has been doing a portrait of Montgo
go too! The grid will make it easier. Look v
what you see. When you have finished you

# trait Painting

le has set up another easel so that you can have a
ely at each square in turn and try to draw exactly
our in your portrait!

# build a snowman!

**To play this game, all you need is a dice and a piece of paper and a pencil. The object of the game is to build a snowman. To start you must throw a 6 to draw the body and then another 6 to draw the head. After that, whatever you throw allows you to draw something – a 4 for an eye and so on. First to finish – wins!**

GET ALONG GANG IN...
MAKING TRACKS!
PART 2
HUGE TRACKS LEADING THIS WAY! TUG ON THE ROPE, PORTIA!
I AM TUGGING, BUT IT'S ALL SLACK!
FOOTPRINTS PASSING EITHER SIDE OF THAT ROCK AND ICE OUTCROP THE GANG HAVE SPLIT UP!
SUDDENLY I DO BELIEVE IN ABOMINABLE SNOW-YETIS! YANK THAT ROPE, BRAKER... WE COULD DO WITH REINFORCEMENTS!
IT LOOKS LIKE WE'RE ON OUR OWN!
FANCY A SNOWBALL FIGHT?
WHIZZ!
NOT WITH MISSILES THAT SIZE... RUN!
WHAT'S THE BIG RUSH, KIDS?
GOOD NEWS BAD NEWS, MAC. WE'VE FOUND YOUR YETI...

BAD NEWS... IT'S FOUND US! AND IT WANTS A SNOWBALL FIGHT!
YIIKES!
FLUMF!
WHAT'S THE MATTER? YOU'RE NO FUN... DON'T WANT TO PLAY!
THWUMP! THOMP!
MEANWHILE, SOME DISTANCE AHEAD...
THE PRINTS HAVE STOPPED AT THIS SHEER ROCK FACE. WHERE DO WE GO FROM HERE?
UPWARDS IF WE CAN... HEAR THAT? COULD BE AN AVALANCHE HEADING THIS WAY!
LEAVE IT TO ME... I SPY A HANDY POINT OF ROCK UP THERE!
BINGO'S BANG ON TARGET AS USUAL... UP WE GO!
ERK! IT WASN'T A ROCK... IT... IT'S THE TOOTH OF A FEAR-FULLY FANGED FIEND!

AND IT'S WOKEN UP!
MEANWHILE BELOW...
YOU CAN'T RUN ANYWHERE NOW... AND I ONLY WANTED FRIENDS TO PLAY WITH!
PICK ON SOMEONE YOUR OWN SIZE!
GROOOAAAH! ROAAR!
POP
YIKES! THE TOOTH'S COME OUT! GOING DOWN!
DONK!
DONK!
NICE OF YOU TO DROP IN!
YAAAY... THE GANG'S ALL HERE. AND NOW IT'S SAFE TO GET A SNAP OF THAT YETI!
DONK!

ROAAR!
MAYBE... BUT NOT OF THAT ONE, MAC! IT'S LOST A TOOTH... AND ITS TEMPER!
HUH... TWO OF THEM!
HETTY... IS IT YOU?
BETTY!
FLUMPH
HAVEN'T SEEN YOU FOR YEARS. BEEN AVOIDING ME?
I CERTAINLY HAVE! ALL THAT ROARING! YOU ALWAYS USED TO HAVE A TEMPER WHEN WE WERE SNOWKIDS!
I WAS ONLY ROARING BECAUSE OF MY TOOTHACHE. HAD IT FOR YEARS UNTIL THESE YOUNGSTERS PULLED THE TOOTH OUT FOR ME!
ANYWAY, I COULDN'T EVER GET NEAR YOUR CAVE FOR THE AVALANCHES!
MY FAULT. TARGET THROWING AT MOUNTAIN PEAKS WITH SNOWBALLS...
YOUR CAMERA, MAC!
YOU'VE GOT YOUR PHOTOS AND THEY'VE GOT THEIR FRIENDSHIP... BRINGING FOLKS TOGETHER IS WHAT THE GET ALONG GANG IS ALL ABOUT!
CLICK!
NO MORE ROARING, NO MORE AVALANCHES!

COME AND SEE MY NEW CAVE, HETTY. IT HAS A WALL TO WALL CARPET - OF SNOW!
WE CAN GET ALONG BACK HOME NOW!
AT LAST SOMEONE TO TELL MY JOKES TO. LIKE... WHAT'S AN ABOMINABLE SNOWMAN'S FAVOURITE FOOD ?
?
WHAT ELSE BUT... SPAG-YETI! HA, HA, HA!
OH, OH... THE GROUND'S SHAKING... TIME TO GO!
HEE, HEE, HEE!
HA! HA! TELL US ANOTHER! HEE! HEE! HEE!
THIS IS FUN!
NOW THEY'RE BOTH ROARING... ROARING WITH LAUGHTER!
LOOK AT THOSE HAPPY FACES, SUNNY SMILES. NO ONE WILL EVER BELIEVE THE PHOTO'S FOR REAL!
WHAT'S UP, MAC?
THE FIRST EVER PHOTO OF THE DREADED, ABOMINABLE SNOWMEN!
A SORT OF "YETI-ALONG GANG, EH?

Skid! On 2!
Skid! On 2!
Miss a go!
Miss a go!
Miss a go!
On 3!
On 3!
Finish!
Finis
LAMPITT & BRADSHAW

# SKI RACE!

Team up with a member of the gang to play an exciting ski race. All you need is a dice and counters. To start you must throw a 6.

# THE FOOTBALL GAME

**The Gang accepted the Greenstreet Hill Mob's challenge to a game of football... and then realised that most of them had no idea how to play!**

"You young hooligans! When I catch hold of you...!" An angry Mr Hoofnagel ran out of his Ice-Cream Emporium and Sweet Shoppe, waving a broom over his head. The Greenstreet Hill Mob were faster and easily dodged past Mr Hoofnagel as he swiped at them with his broom. "Nyaaa! Silly old goat! Can't catch us!" they sang as they pulled ugly faces and danced around him.

Suddenly, the Mob found themselves falling flat on their backs as they stepped on marbles that had been scattered under their feet.

"Whoops! Did I do that?" chuckled Bingo, standing with the rest of the Gang and holding up an empty bag. "Sorry. My marbles escaped!"

"Gurr! You did that on purpose!" snarled Brick, the badger leader of the Mob. "I'll bash you fer that!"

"You won't be bashing anyone!" said an angry voice behind them. It was Officer Growler. "I want a report on what's been going on."

"These rogues came into my shop with their football and started kicking it around. They knocked over all my sweet stalls!" complained Mr Hoofnagel, pointing to the Mob.

"Don't worry," said Montgomery kindly. "We'll tidy up for you."

"Huh! Do-gooders!" snarled Brick, glaring at the Gang.

Officer Growler shook a finger at Brick. "At least they're a helpful gang, not like your rough lot. If I wasn't so busy, I'd go and see your parents. So behave – or else!"

When Growler had gone, Brick turned on the Gang. "It's your fault, interfering goodies! We could have got clean away if not for your rotten gang!"

Rocco took offence at this. "Our Gang's better than your Mob any day!"

"Prove it!" challenged Sharky, Brick's right-hand racoon. "Our Mob could lick your Gang easily!"

Montgomery thought for a moment. "Since you're so interested in football, let's hold a match to decide which gang is best."

"Done!" agreed Brick. "We'll meet in the park in three days' time." The Mob then wandered off to find some more mischief to get up to.

Bernice frowned. "Maybe I should have mentioned this before, but I can't play football," she admitted. "Every time I kick a ball, I fall over."

"I'm not much better," agreed Braker.

"Nor me," said Flora.

"In that case, we'd best start practising," decided Rudyard. "Otherwise they'll beat us and be the best gang in Green Meadow."

"SHOOT, FLORA! SHOOT!" screamed Zipper excitedly. Flora, hobbling unsteadily up the field in the football boots she had borrowed from Rocco, kicked at the football in front of her.

"I kicked it!" she cheered happily as the ball dribbled to a stop a few paces from her foot.

"Er, well done," Dotty praised her friend to give her some encouragement.

"A one-legged parrot could do better!" Zipper mumbled crossly but he shut-up when Dotty gave him a icy stare.

Rudyard and Montgomery were trying to teach Braker how to head a football.

"Jump high like I showed you," Montgomery told him, throwing the ball into the air.

Braker leapt up... and crashed back down on top of Montgomery and Rudyard.

**WHUMP!**

"**GASP!** I think you missed," groaned Montgomery.

"Missed? It was a direct hit – and I've got the bruises to prove it!" Rudyard grumbled, staggering to his feet.

"I did tell you I wasn't very good," apologised Braker. "Perhaps you shouldn't include me in the team?"

"Do I have to play?" Bernice asked Bingo, Lolly and Portia as they made her take another shot at the goal. "Couldn't I be the submarine or something?"

"You mean *substitute*," Lolly corrected her. "And we might need you on the day, so you have to practise. The reputation of the Gang is at stake."

Bernice kicked at the ball as hard as she could. Bingo, in goal testing his goalkeeping skills, dived as something flashed past him. "I've got it!" he cried triumphantly as he held

something in his hands. Portia burst out laughing. "You batty beaver! That's Lolly's football boot. It came off her foot when she kicked. She missed the ball altogether!"

"You lot are hopeless," moaned Rocco angrily. "I'm off to train on my own."

"Me too," agreed both Zipper and Woolma. The others felt the same and soon only Montgomery and Dotty were left.

"This is hopeless," Dotty sighed. "We're the only ones in the team now. How are the two of us going to take on the whole Greenstreet Hill Mob and win?"

Now a lesson that the Gang had learned many times before, but sometimes forgot in the heat of the moment, was that things worked out best when they stuck together. Bingo was already discovering this for himself.

**WHUMPH!**

"Oooyah! That's the fifth time my silly ball has bounced off the wall and whacked me in the face!" he bellowed crossly, rubbing his sore nose. "I think it was more fun practising with the rest of the Gang after all."

Woolma, Lolly and Bernice were attempting to pass a ball to one another. "To me!" cried Bernice, waving to Lolly who had control of the ball.

**WALLOP!**

Lolly kicked the ball hard and it sailed over Bernice's head.

**SMMAAASSH!**

It went through a window of Lolly's dad's sweet factory.

"No pocket-money for you for a month!" her dad scolded her. "And no sweets either!" Lolly did feel glum.

"I'm going off this stupid football lark," she groaned.

"Come on, let's go and listen to Montgomery's advice," suggested Woolma. "Like we should have done in the first place."

Zipper, Rocco and Rudyard were out jogging to strengthen their legs. "We'll be the fastest players on the field!" chuckled Rudyard.

**KRUMMP!**

The boys were so busy chatting, they didn't see the chimney sweep coming out of a house with a sack full of soot, until they ran into him. The sweep dropped the sack which landed on the boys. The soot fell out all over them.

"We may be the fastest players," spluttered Rocco. "But we'll also be the dirtiest!"

Flora and Braker appeared at that moment. "I kicked my ball into the river and lost it," Braker explained. "And Flora tried heading the ball and bashed her head on the branch of a

tree instead. So we're going back to Montgomery and Dotty."

"Good idea," agreed Zipper, dusting the soot off his smart, red tracksuit. "I was going to suggest that myself!"

Montgomery and Dotty were pleased to see their friends. Soon everyone was practising hard together. Three days later they were all grinning confidently as they stood outside the Caboose, dressed in their football outfits and boots.

"All that practising has done wonders. Even I can play football now," Braker beamed happily. "Teamwork was the answer after all."

"Yeah, the Greenstreet Hill Mob won't stand a chance," agreed Portia. But the Gang's discussion was overheard by Sharky, who hurried off to tell Brick.

"**OOORFLE!** That's cheating!" Portia squealed as her feet were kicked from under her by one of the Mob's players. The player ignored her protests and ran towards the Gang's goal. Bingo steadied himself to catch the ball when suddenly Brick charged into him, knocking him over and the ball dribbled into the goal.

"**GOAL**!" cheered Sharky. "Three-nil!"

"This is hopeless," groaned Braker. "The Mob have been bashing us to pieces since the game began."

This, in fact, was Brick's master-plan. When Sharky had told him how good the Gang were, he decided that the only way to beat them was to cheat by playing dirty.

"Squash 'em, pound 'em, marmalise 'em!" he ordered his players and that was what they were now doing.

"The trouble is, we didn't think to bring a referee, so there's no-one to keep them to the rules," Montgomery said after he had been squashed between two big bulldogs from the Mob's team. "If we don't come up with an idea, we're going to lose the match after all."

At half-time, the Mob were leading eight goals to none. The Gang were feeling very depressed as they hobbled back into the changing-rooms.

"Hey, where's Montgomery going? asked Woolma. She watched her friend run out of the park ground. "Don't say he's deserting us?"

Seconds before the second-half,

Montgomery returned with Officer Growler in tow.

"All proper football games have refs," Montgomery explained to Brick who had demanded to know what Growler was doing there. "Officer Growler has agreed to be ours."

Brick's face dropped. "B-B-But..." he stammered, and then shut up when Growler looked sternly at him.

To the Gang's delight, the Mob were too scared of Growler to cheat anymore. They dared not foul the Gang in case Growler reported them to their parents. This gave the Gang the opportunity to show what they could really do. The Mob's faces dropped as the Gang's teamwork ran rings around them.

"**GOAL!**" cheered Zipper as he scored his sixth goal in as many minutes.

"I've scored!" yelled a delighted Portia, moments later. It wasn't long before the Gang had caught up with the Mob's lead and when Braker put the ball in the back of the next, seconds before the end of the match, the Gang had won 20-8.

"**WE ARE THE CHAMPIONS!**" they sang as they did a lap of honour around the park. The Mob went slouching off, crushed at being beaten by their worse enemies.

"Well done," praised Officer Growler as he handed the Gang a small winners' cup he had brought along to present to the winners. "I don't like cheats. I'm glad you won!"

"So am I!" grinned Montgomery. "You could say I get a real **KICK** out of beating the Mob! Ha! Ha!

MONTGOMERY'S BALLOON!
A
Montgomery has designed this

as shown below.
cup. First trace around the balloon shape and trace it twice onto a piece of card – one with the slot at the top, one at the bottom as shown.
Cut the shapes out taking care to cut slots. Now trace the drawing of Montgomery onto both sides of each piece of card and colour.
Pierce the holes at the 4 corners and thread pieces of string or wool through them and attach. Now take the paper cup, make four
holes in it at the top and tie pieces of string through the holes. Make a hole in the top of the balloon and hang it up!

# GET ALONG GANG IN... DISAPPEARING ACT!*

KEEP OFF THE GRASS
WONDER IF I'VE GOT THE MAGIC TOUCH AND CAN MAKE THAT SIGN DISAPPEAR? **ALAKAZAAM!**
DIDN'T WORK! AND HERE COMES WOOLMA LAMB! SHE'LL WANT THE TEN PENCE I BORROWED FROM CLUB FUNDS TO GO TO THE MAGIC SHOW, I BET!
KEEP OFF THE GRASS
HUH? SHE'S WALKED RIGHT PAST! AS THOUGH SHE HADN'T SEEN ME!
PERHAPS I HELD THE WAND THE WRONG WAY ROUND. PERHAPS THE MAGIC END WAS POINTING AT ME. P- PERHAPS I'M INVISIBLE!
DONK!!
OO! I HATE WINDY WEATHER! MY LOVELY LONG LASHES GET ALL TANGLED TOGETHER. I CAN'T SEE ANYTHING!
MEANWHILE...
PORTIA UP AHEAD WONDER IF SHE CAN HELP ME?
HUUH?

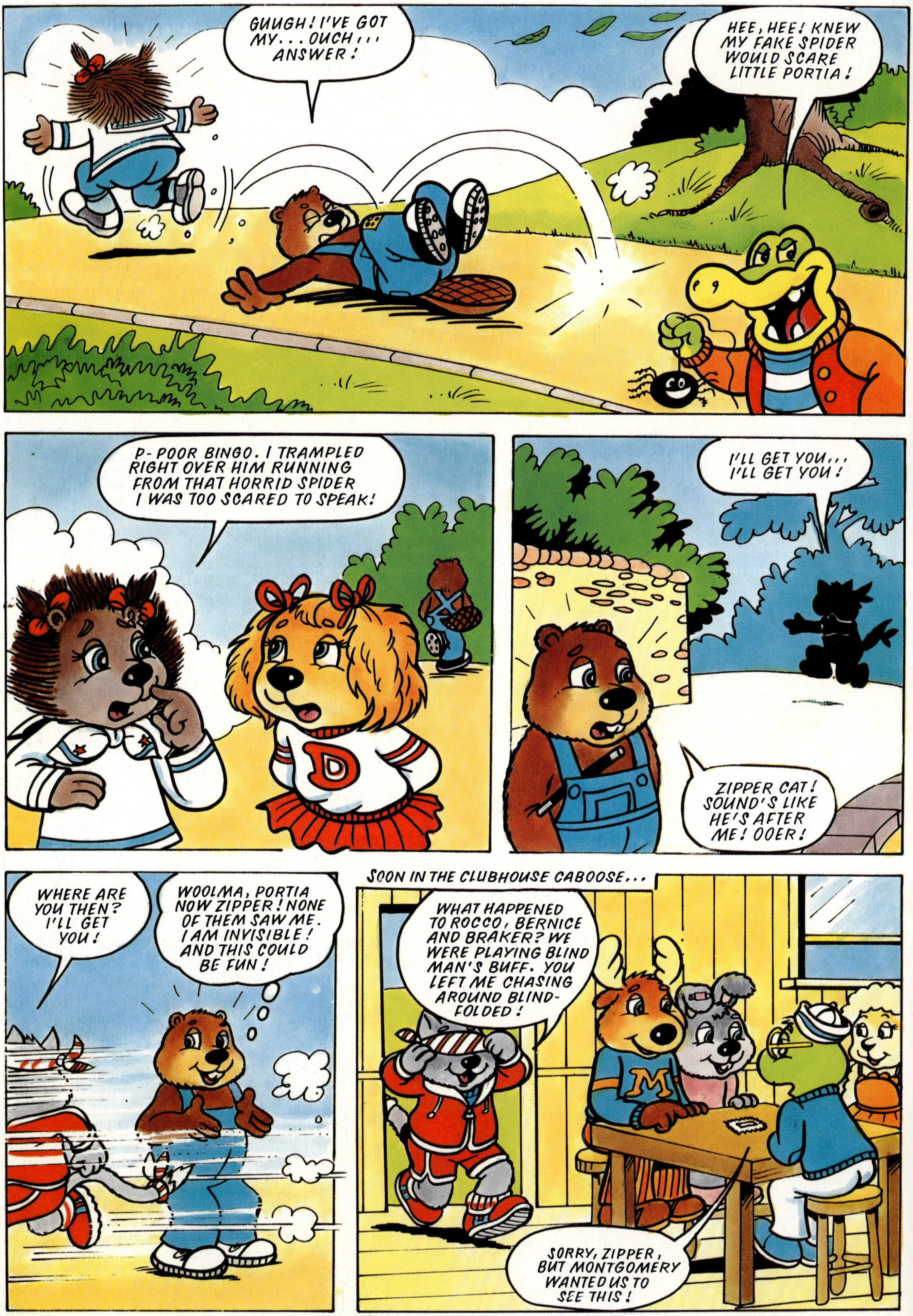
GUUGH! I'VE GOT MY... OUCH... ANSWER!
HEE, HEE! KNEW MY FAKE SPIDER WOULD SCARE LITTLE PORTIA!
P-POOR BINGO. I TRAMPLED RIGHT OVER HIM RUNNING FROM THAT HORRID SPIDER I WAS TOO SCARED TO SPEAK!
I'LL GET YOU... I'LL GET YOU!
ZIPPER CAT! SOUND'S LIKE HE'S AFTER ME! OOER!
WHERE ARE YOU THEN? I'LL GET YOU!
WOOLMA, PORTIA NOW ZIPPER! NONE OF THEM SAW ME. I AM INVISIBLE! AND THIS COULD BE FUN!
SOON IN THE CLUBHOUSE CABOOSE...
WHAT HAPPENED TO ROCCO, BERNICE AND BRAKER? WE WERE PLAYING BLIND MAN'S BUFF. YOU LEFT ME CHASING AROUND BLIND-FOLDED!
SORRY, ZIPPER, BUT MONTGOMERY WANTED US TO SEE THIS!

A VERY RARE STAMP FOR OUR GET ALONG GANG COLLECTION!
QUIETLY DOES IT. I'LL MAKE THEM JUMP...THINK-ING THAT TABLE'S HAUNTED!
AND...
WHOOO-OOO!
ERK! THE TABLE...THE STAMP!
IT'S BLOWN OUT OF THE WINDOW! EVERYONE AFTER THAT STAMP...IT'S WORTH A LOT OF MONEY!
OH-OH! THAT WAS A STUPID TRICK!
THEY'VE GONE IN THE WRONG DIRECTION, THE STAMP'S LANDING ON THAT POST-RAM'S CAP! I'LL LEND A HAND– INVISIBLE OF COURSE!
BUMP!
SORRY, BET YOU DON'T KNOW WHAT HIT YOU! LUCKY FOR ME!
WHAT... GUUGH!
SPLAT!
WHAT... YIKES!
GOT IT BEFORE IT COULD BLOW AWAY AGAIN!

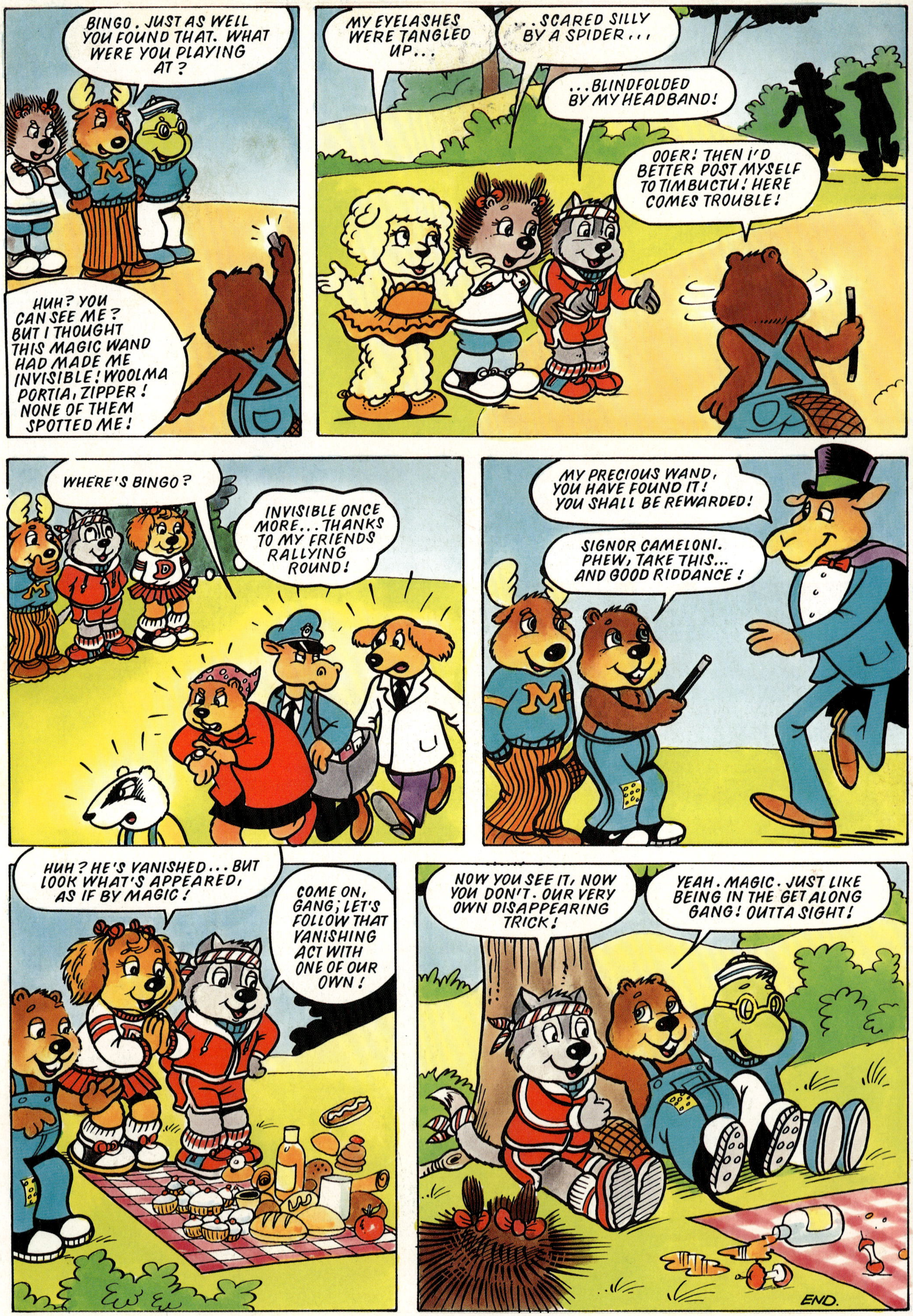
BINGO. JUST AS WELL YOU FOUND THAT. WHAT WERE YOU PLAYING AT?
HUH? YOU CAN SEE ME? BUT I THOUGHT THIS MAGIC WAND HAD MADE ME INVISIBLE! WOOLMA PORTIA, ZIPPER! NONE OF THEM SPOTTED ME!
MY EYELASHES WERE TANGLED UP...
...SCARED SILLY BY A SPIDER...
...BLINDFOLDED BY MY HEADBAND!
OOER! THEN I'D BETTER POST MYSELF TO TIMBUCTU! HERE COMES TROUBLE!
WHERE'S BINGO?
INVISIBLE ONCE MORE... THANKS TO MY FRIENDS RALLYING ROUND!
MY PRECIOUS WAND, YOU HAVE FOUND IT! YOU SHALL BE REWARDED!
SIGNOR CAMELONI. PHEW, TAKE THIS... AND GOOD RIDDANCE!
HUH? HE'S VANISHED... BUT LOOK WHAT'S APPEARED, AS IF BY MAGIC!
COME ON, GANG; LET'S FOLLOW THAT VANISHING ACT WITH ONE OF OUR OWN!
NOW YOU SEE IT, NOW YOU DON'T. OUR VERY OWN DISAPPEARING TRICK!
YEAH. MAGIC. JUST LIKE BEING IN THE GET ALONG GANG! OUTTA SIGHT!
END.

# TRAFFIC QUIZ!

**How well do you know your Highway Code? Officer Growler has set up a quiz to find out. What do each of the signs mean? To make things easier, he has given you a choice of answers. Now check with a copy of the Highway Code and see how many you have right!**

# BRAKER'S ? X-WORD

## Clues!

### Down

1. She is a lamb.
2. The yellow of an egg.
3. He is a lion.
4. She is a bear.
5. The ice-cream seller.
6. ——— "Bet-It-All" Beaver.
7. Fried ———
8. Dotty has two in her hair.

### Across.

1. She is a squirrel.
2. A very spikey girl.
3. Where the Gang meet!
4. Opposite to good.
5. Opposite to stop.
6. Take the 'D' off bed.
7. He is a rabbit.
8. Catchum's chum.
9. Where the Gang live.

LAMPITT & BRADSHAW.